What Do I Do Now?

Beginner's guide to walking with Jesus

Ron Buch

Partnership
Publications

Partnership Publications
www.h2hp.com

What Do I Do Now?

by Ron Buch

© 2015 by Ron Buch

Partnership Publications
A Division of House to House Publications
www.H2HP.com

ISBN 10: 0-9962924-5-4
ISBN 13: 978-0-9962924-5-0

Printed in the United States of America

Contents

Introduction

This book is written to help to those who have experienced the "new birth" spoken of by Jesus Christ in the Bible (John 3:3-8).

After 35 years of following Jesus and His teachings, I was inspired to make some short notes on the things I've learned. This book is not meant to be a substitute for personal study of the Bible, but rather a reference guide to help new followers find their place in the family of God. As we follow the Holy Spirit and spend time in the presence of the God, He will illuminate more and more truths to help us love and live wholeheartedly for Him.

I have embraced the Word of God as my manual for life, without doubting but expecting that if I were to be on earth long enough I would "come to the unity of the faith and the knowledge of the Son of God, to a perfect man, to the measure of the stature of the fullness of Christ" (Ephesians 4:13 NKJV).

Enjoy the life of God while you are still in your body. Peace, joy, and love are fruits that all can see. My suggestion is live ONE day at a time. Do the basics outlined in this book. Don't rush. Be found listening more than speaking. Live this new life one-day-at-a-time with passion. Follow Jesus with all your heart. Your testing time on earth will be fruitful and glorifying to the God who created you for His pleasure. Become a worshipper of Jesus and fulfill His desire to become one with Him and the Father (John 14:23).

Take the time to look up the scripture references. Allow the Word of God to bear witness in your spirit by His Spirit that you are a child of God (Romans 8:16). Read three to four scriptures before and after each reference given so you can see it in context with the remainder of the chapter. Ask the Holy Spirit to give you understanding of His Word (Ephesians 1:17-19 and 1 John 2:27).

My "Born Again" Experience

In 1978 I was a third-year college student who was disenfranchised with the world around me: its smell of unfairness, materialism, and hatred. Although I had gone through catechism classes as a pre-teen and knew Bible stories, I had no significant spiritual experience. I struggled through a life of addiction and depression until I embraced eastern thought and religions. I followed a guru and began a seven-day-a-week commitment to "find God," which would have eventually led me to a mountain in Tibet in search of truth.

I left college and embarked on a two-month journey by meeting with a local ashram daily and emptying myself in search of God. The guru I was following spoke of the "kingdom of God within" and said that he had the same spirit that was in Jesus 2,000 years before. He claimed that spirit had gone from body to body since that time and now resided within him.

My spiritual acuity was lacking, but I was pursuing God and very driven and focused in that effort.

At one point in the second month I said a wild prayer to God, from a sincere heart, asking Him to show me the way if what I was doing was not correct.

Within two weeks my recently "born again" mother asked me to meet her and my father at the home of a devout Christian family for dinner. I took my altar, pictures of my guru, and literature with me for worship.

While eating dinner this man looked at me and said, "Ron, Jesus Christ is Lord. He is the Lord of all Lords and King of all Kings."

Instantly I realized that both my guru and I were lower than the God of the Bible. I was born of the Spirit that hour as I said in my heart it is the Truth. I bowed my knee to this Lord. I came to His Kingdom through His Lordship. Some come through fear of judgment and eternal damnation; some come to Him through His LOVE. Some come by calling on His name (Acts 2:21) out of desperation and hopelessness.

Because I did not know what the "new birth experience" was, since I had not been taught this by teachers of the Bible (pastor, Sunday school teachers), I did not understand what had happened to me. All I knew was that I no longer followed guru Maharaji. I felt completely peaceful inside. I ripped up my pictures of him and destroyed that altar.

I began my search for the seven-day-a-week church. I had crossed over the bridge to eternal life. The old way of sin was left behind.

My life in Jesus had just begun and I needed to know what to do next. It would have been nice to have a mini-book like this to start out in the right direction, but God took care of me immediately by surrounding me with mature Christians (followers of Christ). I embraced His call to follow.

Who Are You?

In John 3:3, Jesus explained that we must be born again to see the kingdom of heaven and born of water and the spirit to enter into the kingdom of heaven (verse 5). The "new birth" or "born again" experience occurs when we believe in our heart that Jesus is Lord, that He was raised from the dead, and is able to save our soul (Romans 10:9-10).

When someone talks about being "saved" they are speaking about this process. It occurs when you believe in your heart and confess with your mouth.

The salvation of God is evident by the witness inside that we have eternal life since we believe in the Son and His deliverance from sin and its consequences (1 John 5:10-12). People will see that you are different when this happens to you. This means we live forever (eternal life) if we are "in Him" and stay there. Sin cannot kill us anymore if we are "dead and our life is hid in Christ" (Romans 6:11, 22; Colossians 2:13, 3:3).

"Therefore if any man be in Christ, he is a new creature (creation), old things are passed away; behold all things are become new" (2 Corinthians 5:17). See yourself as NEW and act like it. It is not hard when the Spirit of God lives in you (Romans 8:9-11) because nothing can separate you from His love (Romans 8:38-39).

After we become part of the family of God, we must move on into obedience (1 John 2:3-5, 5:1-2) and show our love for Him.

This interesting new existence of being in the same body but having the soul with its intellect, which must be renewed (Romans 12:2) to the things of God, may feel strange at first. We are born again in our spirit. All things are new on the inside. The memories are still there of our life before Christ. Our body still wants to express what our emotions and mind lust for. But we have become the temple of the Holy Spirit. Things will never be the same (1 Corinthians 3:16-17). God has come to live inside of us (1 John 4:15). We are sealed with His Holy Spirit (2 Corinthians 1:22, Ephesians 1:13-14, 4:30).

Quit acting like you are the same person. The greatest miracle on earth has happened in your body. Jesus has brought salvation to your soul, forgiven you of your sin, and washed you by His Word. This is now the day of your salvation (2 Corinthians 6:2, 1 Peter 1:3-5). Depart from the life of sin and embrace the gift of God—ETERNAL LIFE (Romans 6:23).

Body, Soul, and Spirit

It is important to understand who we are as a created being. God made us in His image (Genesis 1:26-27). That is why Satan hates us so much. The real icing on the cake is that we look like Jesus (Romans 8:29). We have everything we need to succeed through Him (2 Peter 1:3-4).

You are a conqueror (Romans 8:37), an overcomer (1 John 5:4-5), and you can do all things through Christ who strengthens you (Philippians 4:13).

Now let's talk about our three-part being and get a better understanding of who we are. We are a spirit, who is recognized by our soul (emotions, intellect, and will) and dwells in a body on earth (1 Thessalonians 5:23).

It is important to recognize the difference between the incorruptible place that our new spirit dwells in with the Holy Spirit (1 John 3:9).

Consider it the Holy of Holies where God dwells and no sin approaches. No sin thoughts or deeds come from that place. It is the deepest place of our existence. It is where we hear from God, communicate with Him righteously, and get our direction in life.

Our mind has not been so holy. It is the part of our soul that must be cleansed and renewed to comprehend the Truth (Romans 12:2). At times it is at war with God (Romans 8:6-7). The Word of God (Bible) should be used:

Read aloud to yourself to inspire the connection of your spirit and mind to come into harmony with God (Romans 10:17).

Many times I have a "gut knowing" about the Truth that overrides my conscience thought. I have learned to follow that leading and allow God to show me in His Word what He wants me to know. When my mind has understanding it is easier to allow my soul, through the strength of my will, to follow the will of God for my life and not worry about the consequences. We should locate our spirit (Job 32:8, Proverbs 20:27, Zechariah 12:1, and 1 Corinthians 2:11) and commune with God daily (1 Corinthians 14:2, 14, 15) to find the greatest place of peace on earth for our soul (John 14:27, Philippians 4:7).

Developing your new spirit man is like exercising a muscle. The more activity you give to it (worship, praise, faith, prayer) and the more Word of God that you ingest, the stronger you will get.

At the beginning you are a child, drinking milk and needing to learn the basics of the kingdom (Hebrews 6:1-2), but you must move on to maturity and take meat to become effective beyond your own journey and fulfill the kingdom purposes that God has given to you as a part of the body of Christ (1 Corinthians 3:2, Hebrews 5:12-14, 1 Peter 2:2). Over time our spirit man must become the greatest part of our being.

Initally when we are born again, our spirit is the smallest portion of our three-part being. We are generally dominated by what our body wants based on the lust of our carnal nature. Self-seeking, lover of self, all-for-me attitudes are normal fleshly or carnal attributes. You will find that your new spirit man knows that this is at war with God and cannot please Him (Romans 8:5-13). So you will come to the daily knowledge of carnal (flesh) versus spirit and get the choice to grow by the Word of God.

The Holy Spirit leads or moves deeper into the stubbornness in your soul (will, mind, emotions) that fights against the Truth. Because salvation includes deliverance from sin, you will always be able to choose the path of freedom from the strength of your inner man in each situation you face. Of course that is only if your spirit man is running the show.

If your mind, emotions, will, or body are running the show, you will face difficulties as you oppose Jesus (The Way, The Truth, and The Life) and attempt to be god of your way (Romans 13:2, 2 Timothy 3:5-9, James 4:6-7).

The sooner you submit to God in every area of your life, the better it will be. Anarchy lives in the old man, rebellion is its cousin, and our flesh thinks it can get away with things like we used to. This is faulty thinking and will be exposed by the Spirit of Truth who now lives in you.

Move towards peace with God, obey His commandments from a willing spirit and your mind will come along for the ride. Flesh versus spirit—rebellion versus obedience—death versus life. Guess who wins? You do if you submit body, soul, and spirit to the Lord of the living, Jesus Christ. It gets easier as your spirit man grows. Let's move into how we do that.

Old Man and New Man

After we understand that we are spirit, soul, and body, we must focus our efforts on spiritual rather than carnal or worldly existence (Romans 8:6, 8-11). This doesn't mean we become no earthly good for the Kingdom of God. It is about what we deem most important in our life (Matthew 6:19-21, 33, 7:7-8, 14; Colossians 3:1-2).

Every day we make choices that honor or dishonor our Lord. Let's look at where these choices come from that our will puts into place.

As a new Christian the battle rages between the old and the new you. The old man was crucified with Christ, that the body of sin (where sin can grow and operate from) might be destroyed, that henceforth we should not serve sin (Romans 6:6). The old you has died. Dead humans don't have the ability to speak or run things from the grave. Neither do you, unless your will gives permission to do it.

Herein do we find the greatest dilemma of a newborn human. We must willfully choose righteousness (a right standing with God) by the obedience of our will to serve and live with God on earth (Galatians 5:16, 17, 24; 1 John 3:24). We must reckon ourselves to be dead indeed to sin but alive unto God through Jesus Christ our Lord (Romans 6:7, 11)

The new man (Ephesians 4:23-24) must be put on (the Greek word means to be clothed with). Our mind must be renewed. According to the Greek interpretation, that means the whole course of life now flows in a different direction. It is a daily act of our will to stop sinning and choose God's will because we are born of Him and "do not practice, commit, perform sin" (1 John 3:9). We obey His commandments and break the cycle of sin. No longer do we call ourselves sinners but rather children of God, lovers of God, followers of the Truth.

How hard is this really? In the beginning of my new life with Christ, I struggled with sin and the thoughts and temptations of it. I discovered that God's grace was more than enough for overcoming my daily life of trials and tribulations.

Remember that we will overcome if our focus remains on what Christ has done for us. This new creation (new man) is the only one who can win the battle with the enemy. The old man already was judged with death for sin (Romans 6:33) and cannot be resurrected for another try at it.

See yourself as "complete in Him" and seated in heavenly places with Christ and this world will not have a grip on you (Ephesians 2:6; Colossians 2:10, 4:12).

Our struggles with sin will ALWAYS be when the old man is allowed to think, speak, and cause our will to act in a manner that is disrespectful to God. This disobedience causes sin to be acceptable in our mind for a moment but will cause us to have difficulty entering into His Presence apart from the covering and forgiveness of Jesus. It is our choice.

The definition of sin is to know to do good and not do it (James 4:17). Thank God He is faithful and just to forgive us of all our sin if we confess it. Repent from the deeds of the old man and receive cleansing from all acts of unrighteousness (1 John1:9). God the Father sees us as the new man, living in harmony with Holy Spirit, and covered by the blood of His Son.

We need to make sure we forgive ourselves and get loose from the guilt and shame of the old man and his deeds. Declaring daily that we are dead and our life is hid with Christ in God reminds us who we are in Christ Jesus.

Keep Yourself

Now that you know who you are and who you were, it is a good time to work on "how do I do this." Many new Christians talk too much about sin and its affect on their life. It's like being around an ex-addict who can't stop trying to talk themselves into getting high. If you think it is an option, then you will do it.

Jesus teaches that from the "abundance of the heart the mouth speaks" (Matthew 12:33-37). We are "snared by the words of our mouth" and confession will bring possession if we believe in our heart and willfully act it out past our declaration of it (Proverbs 6:2, 18:7, 21; Mark 11:23-24). This works for good or for evil "for death and life are in the power of the tongue."

You became "born again" by believing in your heart and confessing with your mouth (Romans 10:9-10). Begin to listen to what comes out of your mouth. As you mature, don't allow wrong beliefs that come from your mind make it out the door of your mouth. Keep yourself out of trouble with God and Satan by honestly looking into your motives and dealing with it at that level. Keep yourself and the wicked one WILL NOT TOUCH YOU (1 John 5:18). If you believe this truth, you will act accordingly in your freedom walk with Christ. More Word = More Victory. Satan and his kingdom do not dominate you anymore. This is a confession that will stand the test of time and help you keep yourself protected.

Now that your mouth is not causing you trouble, let's look into other areas that you can work on keeping yourself. Forgiveness is essential for staying clean before God since His entire plan of salvation is based on it.

Daily we should be listening to our conscience and the Holy Spirit. Respond to the Father by asking for forgiveness when actions and beliefs do not line up with His Word.

The Father has put everything into the hands of Jesus. He is our substitute, our covering, the atoning sacrifice for sin. He gives us forgiveness for our transgressions that deserve death (Roman 3:25, 6:23; Ephesians 5:25-26; 1 John 2:1, 2; 4:10). Staying forgiven is a key element to "keeping yourself."

Many Christians search for that initial euphoria of feeling clean, like when they first got forgiven by Jesus at salvation. You need to know that you are always forgiven when you clean up daily. Over the years I have found that the best way is to daily stay in fellowship with the Light and be covered by the blood (1 John 1:7). In fact, do it every minute of your life, every breath of your life, and sin will not so easily beset you.

Never let the sun go down on your anger or sin (Ephesians 4:26). Being forgiven by God is the most important lifestyle you can live. Don't forget to forgive yourself since God has already done it.

If you "keep yourself" by being quick to forgive, quick to repent, and vigilant to deal with what your conscience is making a point about, then you will have great success (Joshua 1:8). Base these discoveries on the Word of God. Simple everyday "walking in the light" as I would call it.

We can enjoy the benefit of Jesus, who is the light of the world as He allows us to experience His glory (light) by this process of continuous exposure that reveals dark areas of our heart (Isaiah 60:19, Proverbs 4:18-19, Matthew 5:16, John 8:12, 2 Corinthians 4:4; 1 John 1:7; Revelation 21:24).

Walking in the light will result in fellowship with God, other believers, and the world that so desperately needs to see this fruit in human form.

Jesus was not of this world and neither are you now that you are a new creation. Because our home is in heaven, we must separate ourselves from the world although we still live in it. This sanctification, which according to the Greek means to separate from profane to holy, is done by the Holy Spirit through revelation of the Word of God (Jesus). The Holy Spirit works within as much as we allow him.

How important is "thy will be done on earth as it is in heaven?" Give your will to do His Will. Be sanctified by Christ, and walk in this light so that you glorify the God who saved your soul. Others will see Him in you. This "keeping yourself" produces lots of fruit for others to see and will lead them to believe on the one who sent you. It also makes your time on earth much easier because the wicked one has more trouble getting to you.

More World = More Enemy. There is just no way around it. We cannot sin and say we know God. People know what is right, especially when they are not doing it (John 17:14-19; 2 Corinthians 5:20; Philippians 2:14-16; 1 John 2:15-17). So then we need to keep ourselves from the world.

Faith and Power

Once you are "born again" it is important to follow the path that Jesus laid out for His disciples.

Water baptism, which according to the Greek means immersion, submerge, in the name of Jesus was the practice of the disciples when people were converted to Christianity (Acts 2:38; 10:47-48; 18:8; 19:5). 1 Peter 3:21 explains it as an answer of a good conscience toward God. This outward physical expression of the death, burial, and resurrection in our lives symbolizes our transparency to follow Christ, not being ashamed of His Gospel.

Holy Spirit Baptism: Jesus is the baptizer in this experience (Matthew 3:11; John 1:33). Subsequent to the new birth, Jesus spoke of the "promise of the Father" (Luke 24:49; Acts 1:4; Galatians 3:14). The Comforter (John 14:16-17; 26; 15:26) that will make us witnesses in all the earth. This is the manifestation of His power so we would do "greater works than He did" (John 14:12) by following His pattern of anointing from God (Acts 10:38).

Humans had this experience of receiving power from on high by immersion (spirit baptism) in the following chapters in the Acts of the Apostles after Jesus left earth to go to the right hand of the Father: Acts 1:8;2:1-4; 8:14-19; 9:17; 10:44; 19:1-6. Two times it occurred as they waited for Jesus. Acts 2 describes the experience that happened to the Jews. Acts 10 relates the experience of the Gentiles as the first of this people group. In all other instances, the Holy Spirit baptism was administered by the laying on of hands by people who already had the experience.

My Holy Spirit baptism experience: One month after I was born again, I was hearing about this experience for believers after the new birth and was wondering how to get all that God had for me. I had seen the power of drugs and sin in my life and in others too. The strength of the evil was overwhelming, even without talking about witchcraft or other occult practices, which were supernatural for sure.

If Jesus was King of Kings, then He must have a power package for us to make it through this world with its evil power because this Christian life isn't easy. I knew nothing about the Holy Spirit, God's power, or what the Christian life had to offer. I just wanted everything that God had for me.

One Saturday my temp must have been 104F because I was almost hallucinating with pain. It was quiet at my apartment, but I heard a voice inside of me say, "Go to Peter's house, and he will pray for you and you will be healed." I knew it was the voice of God. I immediately jumped in my 1967 Chevelle and stuck my head out the window as I drove because the car did not have air conditioning. I went to Peter's house fully believing I would be healed.

He answered the door and said, "Wow you look bad." I told him that an inner voice had told me to come to him for prayer (Mark 16:18). Peter prayed for me. It felt as if a metal band that had been tightened on my head around my temple was cut. My fever broke and I was healed instantly.

I was thanking God when Peter asked if I wanted to receive the baptism in the Holy Spirit for power and fire in my life. He knew I wanted this experience because the Holy Spirit told him through a word of knowledge as described in 1 Corinthians 12:8. The word of knowledge shows us the revelation of God in the present. I said yes. Peter laid his hands on me and asked Jesus to baptize me with His Holy Spirit and fire. Immediately I felt power come through Peter's hands and through my body. I started speaking in a language I did not learn (I speak English, German, and had three years of French in high school).

The language I was speaking morphed into more than one language as my mouth was speaking what my spirit, by the Holy Spirit inspiration, was hearing. As the scripture says, I was able to think about what I was saying but did not understand it. All I knew was that I was feeling the most intense power and exhilarating passion for God that could not be explained by anything I had previously experienced in life.

I spoke for twenty straight minutes in other tongues as the Spirit gave me utterance. While I was speaking, I began to believe that if I stopped it would be the end of this power forever. I was surprised that the enemy could try to get me to think that was true, but it was a real battle. Let me tell you, I wasn't stopping for anyone even though I did not know what God's Word said about it. Peter, after twenty minutes of praising God also, finally said to me, "Ron, it's okay. You can stop and breathe. You will be able to do this the rest of your life anytime you want to."

I trusted Peter, because he was the most spiritual person I knew in my first month of following Jesus. I stopped speaking, and then started again to see if it was true. Awesome is all I could think, how awesome Jesus was for giving me His power. I proceeded to speak in tongues as much as possible in the next two to three years because it helped me to overcome attacks in my mind from the enemy. What a great way to shut down outside traffic from hell because my mind was at peace when my spirit was praying to God, praising him, and giving thanks well as 1 Corinthians 14 declares. Praying in the spirit is the most significant tool (edifying, building up myself as described in Jude 20) that Jesus gave to me in my first years that helped me break through the enemy's defenses and strongholds in my life.

As much as possible I have continued to pray at all times in the spirit (in tongues as described in Ephesians 6:18). I do not always know who I am praying for, but I know that my Father in heaven hears me and gives me confidence by His Word that I will always know how to pray (Romans 8:26-27). This Holy Spirit utterance in my life is critical and continues to encourage me in faith as I speak what I hear from Him. Remember, our speaking (confession) is where the power is in this earth and in our life. Speak what God says and you will be in His will, whether by Word or Spirit.

The baptism in the Holy Spirit was just the beginning of my walk in the realm of power by the Spirit. I speak almost every day with my heavenly language. It is important to have a supernatural experience every day of your life. God is supernatural and expects us to stay focused on Him. That is why our deepest fellowship is with Him in the spirit, not by our mind. The enemy will try to keep you earthbound in your thinking, using the circumstances of this world to steer you away from the supernatural.

Run the other way towards Jesus. Build yourself up in faith praying in the Holy Spirit whenever you can. When you don't feel spiritual, and when the world has you down, you need to get back up, go to your quiet place and pray or sing in tongues. You will find your place with Him in heavenly places. It's just that simple. Let your spirit man rule your life.

I have prayed in the spirit (in tongues) for over an hour many times throughout my life. It helps me to stay focused on why I am on earth, to worship and serve my God. Want more faith? Pray in the Spirit. Want more supernatural? Sing in the Spirit. Want clearer direction? Be filled with the Spirit on a daily basis.

The Greek definition of being filled with the spirit gives us a view of constant filling, constant worship, and continuous empowerment from on high. Be baptized in the Holy Spirit, stay immersed in His presence, don't dry out, and you will live the overcoming life on earth. God is a Spirit and they that worship Him must worship Him in spirit and truth (John 4:23-24).

Life of Faith

Abraham is a great example of living by faith, not depending on what he saw. Obviously by now you believe in things you do not see with your eyes, you do not feel with your hands, and cannot smell.

Jesus is at the right hand of the Father, but you know Him. So you have moved from the natural to the spiritual. Stay spiritual and you will have the faith of God. Romans 4:17-25 is a must read for us to understand this life of faith. Abraham was fully persuaded that what God had promised, He was able also to perform (v 21). This is the foundation of our life.

"If God said it in His Word, then I believe it" has become my mantra in this life of faith. He gave us promises in His Word that we can hold Him to (Romans 10:17; 2 Peter 1:4). We must hear the Word for faith to be alive in us first. Blind faith does not exist in the Kingdom of God.

All God-based faith is anchored in His Word. MORE WORD = MORE FAITH. This is a simple recipe for success. Read aloud to yourself and by hearing you will activate your spirit man. He responds to the words of God. Just as God does, faith calls those things that be not as though they were (Romans 4:17). I believe I will live forever because God promised me that through Jesus in His Word. I apply faith, believing not what I see but rather what I know to be truth. Faith says: "I will see the manifestation of what I believe." When I get to heaven, I will no longer need to believe that I will get there because I will be living with Jesus forever (1 Peter 1:5,8-9). Faith has obtained it.

When your father says he will get you a bicycle, you believe him even if you do not have it yet. That is faith. The most powerful force of faith on earth is when we believe what our Father God has said and act like it is already so! The definition of faith in the Bible is the substance of things hoped for, the evidence of things not seen (Hebrews 11:1).

In the beginning of my Christian life, I was like a child who trusted his father. I was willing to believe what God said. He quickly rewarded me with the manifestations of the things I asked Him.

Doubt was not my first choice. Faith is the absence of doubt. In Mark 11:22-24 Jesus explains what it means to have faith in God. When you pray, believe you have received your requests, and you shall have them. In the Greek that verse is worded in the past tense. That reveals the power of faith. When you pray (present requests), believe that God has heard you and has given you what He promised, and it is so (you have received). God is in control of the manifestation or appearance of what He gave you when you believed by faith (and you shall have it).

Welcome to Faith 101 from God's manual for life. If you base your requests on the promises of God in His Word, then you have the strongest position of faith. Faith stops when you receive the manifestation of what you asked for.

The world says the opposite: "seeing is believing," which according to the definition of faith from God's Word is not the truth. Mark 11:23 says that if you do not doubt, your belief in what is not seen will come to pass. Like I said, make sure your prayer is based in the Word (promises) of God.

Child-like faith is very different from mountain-moving faith. This is part of our journey from infant to maturity. Jesus knows how to cause faith to grow in us. He is the author and finisher of our faith (Hebrews 12:2). He is the Word by which all things have been made (John1:1-5, Hebrews 11:3).

Here are some notable faith sayings for you as a believer: Faith comes by hearing and hearing by the Word of God (Romans 10:17). Without faith, it is impossible to please God (Hebrews 11:6). The just shall live by faith (Habakkuk 2:4, Romans1:17, Galatians 3:11, Hebrews 10:38). Faith overcomes the world (1 John 5:4). Faith works by love (Galatians 5:6). Righteousness (a right standing with God) is by faith (Romans 9:30, 10:6). By faith you stand (2 Corinthians 1:4). For we walk by faith not by sight (2 Corinthians 5:7). The Shield of faith (Ephesians 6:16, 1 Thessalonians 5:8) and the prayer of faith (James 5:15) are some great verses to memorize.

The faith message is critical for our development in this Christian life. We will experience testing in this area of faith because it must be proven to the praise, honor, and glory of God (1 Peter 1:7-9).

God is watching over His Word and will accomplish what it was sent to do (Isaiah 55:11, Jeremiah 1:12, Ezekiel 12:25). God will finish what He started in our life if we will believe in His Way.

Word mixed with faith = success. In Hebrews 4:2 we see that it is possible to hear the Word of God and not profit by it. That only happens if faith, our belief in what we hear, is not applied in our hearts.

Being followers of Jesus, our faith must have corresponding action so that our works show what we believe because "faith without works is dead" (James 2:14-26). Let's move on to action.

Act Out Your Faith

Here are some practical ways to follow Jesus in your daily life.

1. Prayer Life

Talk to God daily. Expect that He hears you and speaks to you. Faith will obtain what you need from Him (Matthew 6:5-13, Mark 11:24, John 14:13-14, 15:7, James 1:5-8, 5:13-15, 1 John 5:14-15).

2. Study the Bible

Train your mind to acknowledge the truth. Pray Ephesians 1:17-19 so that your time with God will be fruitful. The Holy Spirit will teach you (John 14:26, 1 John 2:20, 27) as you believe in hope that you "know all things" since you are following Him. Allow God to do what He does best: Love you, grow you up in Him, and show His Word to the world as it is in your mouth. Study to show yourself approved by God (2 Timothy 2:15). Look up the scripture references that appear in this book. Learn the concepts and be able to teach or share with others when they ask you about it (1 Peter 3:15).

I suggest a general reading of the Bible by beginning in the Gospel of John, which describes His love for you. Romans chapters 6-8 record the critical foundational revelation of who we are in Christ. Reading Psalms and Proverbs daily will encourage you in many areas of your life. Ask the Holy Spirit where He wants to show you things. Develop this relationship with the teacher and you will hear from Him (Matthew 7:7-8).

3. Become a Giver

When we first come to Christ we are seriously needy. The migration from taker to giver will begin as your needs are met by your Lord (Philippians 4:19). Take the time to learn about the tithe (10 percent according to Malachi 3:8-12) and offerings, which are above and beyond the giving of the tithe. Giving of your time in service to the Kingdom of God can be done in many ways: serving in the church as an usher, teacher, intercessor, or many other "helps" ministry options.

Give, and it shall be given unto you. (Luke 6:38) talks about how you cannot out give God. Move into the opposite mentality of the world today, which is entitlement, selfishness, and greed. Jesus said it is more blessed to give than to receive (Acts 20:35).

The more you practice giving love through actions of faith, the more you will have abundance in your own life to share with others (John 10:10, 2 Corinthians 9:8).

3. Walk in the Light

Fellowship with the body of Christ as you move from self to community. Forsake not the assembly of ourselves together (Hebrews 10:25). Having fellowship with one another is part of walking in the light and maintaining the blood covering and cleansing from sin (1 John 1:7). 1 Corinthians 12:12-27 and Romans 12:4-8 explain that all members of the body of Christ are important and all are needed for the body to function properly. We need to "locate ourselves" and do what Holy Spirit wants us to do while we are in this body.

Finding God's will for your life and doing it is acting out your faith (James 1:22-25). Be blessed in your doing. Faith always has corresponding action. Believe and act. Fruit will follow (Matthew 7:20, Matthew 13:23, John15:2-8, John15:16), and you will give glory to your Father who is in heaven.

4. Stop/Look/Listen

It is important to spend time quiet enough to hear God speak. The traffic of this world (cares of the world, lust of the eyes, and the pride of life) (Mark 4:19, 1 John 2:16) is too loud and causes us to miss what the still small voice inside our spirit is hearing from God. Meditating on the Word of God (Joshua 1:8, Psalms 1:2, 4:4, 63:6, 119:15, 119:27, 1 Timothy 4:15, Philippians 4:8) produces peace and allows our hearts to be exposed.

Meditation is mulling the Word of God or principles of truth around in your mind as you call on God to give you understanding. Revelation from the Holy Spirit during listening times is crucial for the development of an overcoming lifestyle.

Mary Sanchez-Buch, in her book, *Spiritual Bootcamp for Overcomers,* compares it to a flat TV screen in our life. God shows us things and we can inquire of Him as to what the "Real Deal" is behind that stronghold of sin He is revealing to our conscience mind. As we see and contemplate or meditate about it we see in the mirror of our screen the reflection of who we are. If any sin is on us then we must do something about it.

This is scary for many of us. Being transparent and honest with yourself and God is the beginning of freedom in that area of your life. Many people don't want to be still and know that He is God (Psalm 46:10) because it means we must change to remain in fellowship with the Truth.

Praying in the Holy Spirit (1 Corinthians 14:2, 14, 16, 17) is important in the secret place of your communion with God. Prayer, revelation, and direction will come out of these STOP/LOOK/LISTEN moments of quieting down our mind and hearing from Jesus. Dreams and visions can also happen easier when the world is not blaring and causing us to become sense-oriented (see/touch/taste/smell) and miss God's gentle voice of instruction.

Journal some of these times as the Lord shows you things, speaks to you about the future, and helps you look at the "Real Deal" in your life. Intimacy with God the Father, Son, and Holy Spirit is an act of your will.

Ask, and it will be given to you; seek and you will find, knock and it will be opened to you (Matthew 7:7-8). Draw nigh to God and He will draw close to you (James 4:8). God is ready to talk. What are you waiting for?

5. Be a Worshipper

We will be worshipping God forever, so our time on earth should be the training for this. Worship requires a human to give of themselves in a selfless honor of one greater than themselves. God created us to worship him. The Father is seeking true worshippers (John 4:22-24) who worship Him in SPIRIT and in TRUTH. This is because God is a spirit and we must find that connection with him.

Over the years I have found that one can clearly discern if Christians are spending time "in His presence." Listening to worship music and singing to the Lord is an important part of my successful daily fellowship with God. My spirit man is able to experience the "joy of the Lord" in His presence (Psalms 16:11, 100:2).

Enter into His gates with thanksgiving and into His courts with praise. Be thankful to Him, and bless His name (Psalm 100:4). This is a pattern for fellowship with our Holy God. Be a doer of this Word and He will always accept your sacrifice of praise and worship.

Be a Disciple

Now we get down to where the rubber meets the road. If we know who Jesus is, and who He has made us to be, as noted in previous chapters, then we will understand the basic drive inside for our spirit man to lead our soul and body in complete worship of Him. Although Jesus is no longer on the earth, we show the world who He is and what His message of love is (1 John 4:12) when we follow His commandments (1 John 2:3-4, 5:2-3). We also show Him and the world that we love Him.

Jesus defined discipleship in several ways that really separates out the true believers. In Luke 14:26, 27, 33, Jesus clearly defines forsaking all to follow. What do you need to give up to come in line with this Word? (Matthew 8:21, 16:24).

Clearly stated in 2 Corinthians 5:15, "He died for all, that those who live, should no longer live for themselves, but for Him who died for them and rose again." This is a key spiritual truth that grinds against the carnal nature of humans. Our decisions, on a daily basis, locate us in this struggle of our human will against the will of God.

Wisdom is to see yourself as a follower of the risen one, alive from the dead, and 100 percent committed to the plan, purpose and pursuit of God through Jesus Christ. This follower of God, disciple of Jesus, then goes through life compelled to please God so that at the end of their life they will receive the benefit (Psalms 58:11, Proverbs 16:7, Matthew 16:27, Romans 8:8, 15:3, 1 Corinthians 3:14, 9:7, 2 Corinthians 5:1-10, Colossians 1:10, 3:24, Hebrews 13:21).

"Take up your cross and follow him" (Matthew 16:24-28). Jesus explains the crucified life. Not your own, it is different than what the rest of the world is following (2 Timothy 3:1-6). Being a lover of yourself more than a lover of God will lead you to be a lover of pleasure, money, pride, crazy lust, and other worldly pleasure (Galatians 5:19-21, Ephesians 2:1-3, 2 Peter 2:18-22, 1 John 2:16).

Discipleship or following God is required. Following our plan runs into the wall of rebellion and anarchy if we are not willing to live this consecrated life spoken of in this chapter so far.

Anarchy is defined as the state of society without government or law; lack of obedience to an authority; and confusion and disorder. The spirit of anti-christ is at the heart of anarchy to God's law. If someone has consistent rebellion problems to God's Word and principles for living then Jesus is not Lord of all areas within that person.

Obedience at the deepest level of our heart is all that God is asking for. We, as followers of Christ, must bring all thoughts into captivity to the obedience of Christ (2 Corinthians 10:4-6) and be willing to mortify all that is in us that opposes the truth (Romans 8:13, Colossians 3:5). This is "walking in the light." A disciple takes action to remain a true follower of his master. This is where our personal will determines who we are in light of this Gospel. Who are we following? How committed are we to Jesus as Lord of our life?

Most of us have not been raised in this type of environment. We listened to our parents, but did we follow their teaching? Many people make the shift to following their own plan when they embrace rebellion and begin going down the road to anarchy from the truth. The Light of the glorious gospel can change that (2 Corinthian 4:4, Philippians 2:15, 2 Timothy 1:10) through obedience to our Lord and His teaching. We will then prove what is good, and acceptable, and the perfect will of God (Romans 12:2).

Discipleship, as Jesus defined it, happens when we become radical in our pursuit of righteousness (Matthew 6:33-34), when we give all to Him, stay accountable to the body of Christ, and daily remain faithful as a follower.

Conclusion

Living a righteous life is not as hard as the enemy of your faith keeps trying to make you think it is. It is a daily commitment to seek to follow the Truth with all of your energy, as the Word of God instructs. Having a relationship with a human takes a lot of effort. The more intimate the relationship, the more time and energy it takes to maintain a loving position. So it is with the God who created us for intimate relationship. He wants to spend time with us.

Often I have found that my running around, looking for stimulation, whether it be intellectual, physical, emotional, or sense driven, could have been satisfied in the presence of the Lord. Once we as humans experience the anointing or presence of His glory, then we will stop trying to substitute that experience with a cheap, flash in the pan, high or lustful moment.

As I seek more time with Jesus, I am coming to a better understanding of what King David spoke of when he said "Better is one day in your house than a thousand elsewhere." He knew the presence of the Lord. Yet interestingly enough he still struggled like we do, fighting off sin and the lust of his flesh. The difference is we have experienced the Savior and His great salvation. We are living under the more excellent covenant. We know Messiah.

Here are some tips for having a normal Christian life on earth. Expect to be tried, tested, and opposed as you move from infant to mature adult. Victory will also come, hopefully daily, as you learn to overcome your circumstances and change from who you were yesterday into who Jesus called you to be.

The overcoming lifestyle always stands up when knocked down, keeps himself so the wicked cannot touch him, and expects to get the revelation needed minute by minute to stay in God's presence no matter what the circumstances. Always believes the Truth above the lie, always hopes in the Holy Spirit's education and direction to find the way of escape, always grows. Be quick to repent, slow to anger, and forgive those who need to be forgiven.

Stay forgiven

If an act is under the blood of Christ, if you have asked for forgiveness and gotten it by faith, then it is buried in the depths of the sea and no longer worth talking about. You are in control of your thoughts and will. Forgive yourself. Believe God's Word as He says it. Don't lose trust. If God said it in His Word, then it is so.

Many times we complicate our daily walk by giving too much credit to the devil. Every evil thought or action is not caused by Satan or one of his devils. Many times it is our old man—carnal nature—that needs to be killed. If you are having trouble telling the difference, talk with a more mature Christian than yourself to help you discern sin and the behavior of the sin nature.

Take authority over the devil and his influence and bind or cast him out of your life when that is needed. Build trust with Holy Spirit directed leaders who can show you in the Word how to deal with your stuff. Remember, each of us has a different path where we have come from and where we are going in the Kingdom.

Find out what God's plan is for you and stick to it

Prove what is true and hold on to everything that brings peace. Make sure the Bible says so before you jump into new things. Hang out with people who show the fruit of the Spirit in their lifestyles (Galatians 5:22-23).

Pray, fast, believe, love, and act as if Jesus was coming back today for you. Stay covered by the blood, cleansed by His Word, and faithful to the one who saved your soul. Laugh and cry with those of your family. Treat them like you will be with them forever in heaven. It will change your view.

Do good works whenever you can so as to glorify and honor Jesus on earth until He comes again. Feed the hungry, clothe the poor, and give your life, denying its pleasures and benefits, for the good of others like Jesus did.

Avoid sin on a daily basis by the acts of your will

Be quick to say NO to sin and YES to God. Follow the Holy Spirit by paying attention to what He suggests. This is explained in the book "Spiritual Bootcamp for Overcomers" by Mary Sanchez Buch. The section "What's on your screen" explains how the Holy Spirit speaks to our spirit in the language of the spirit, communicating directly with our spirit man.

The problem in human existence is that our soul (intellect, emotions, and will) distorts the communication from within. As you grow in your Christian walk, you will become better at hearing the voice of Holy Spirit as guide, attorney, counselor, and leader. During our time on earth, the Holy Spirit exposes all sin and shows us the exit strategy through change.

If we watch what He is showing us "on our screen, we can put the hand of our will to the process and come out the other side in righteousness (a right standing with God). The screen idea is a way to explain how we discern the communication from Holy Spirit. He reveals the light of His Truth. We handle the information through our soul, with a high emphasis on the mind or intellect as the conscious point of reference.

Our mind needs to be constantly renewed to come in line with the Truth. Sometimes the "screen" is so vivid that we instantly understand the message. Other times, when we are entangled in carnal living, driven by our senses and circumstances, God gives us dreams or visions to help us out. He will take it so far, as seen in the Old Testament, that if we can't hear Him He will send a donkey to speak (Numbers 22:27-30). All who are "born" of God know their shepherd's voice, have the "witness of the Spirit" inside, and lack no holy communication because we "have all things pertaining to godliness (2 Peter 1:3). This is a state of complete confidence that God loves us, talks to us through His Spirit, and has it all under control in our life through the authority and Lordship of Jesus Christ. "Our spirit bears witness with the Holy Spirit that we are the sons of God" (Romans 8:16).

Personally I have known the "witness of the Spirit" in my spirit man at the depth of my being, as the most undeniable and unable to be questioned or compromised place on earth. Many times in my Christian life I "knew" inside without need for reasoning exactly what the perfect will of God was in the situation I was facing. This knowing was foundational, unable to be explained or justified. This inward witness is always my place of rest. I try to rest in these places of peace and avoid intellectual wrangling that could disrupt my soul.

"What if?" doesn't always lead to higher consciousness with the creator God we know as Jesus. We are able to know some things without over analyzing to the point of losing peace.

For instance, I have never questioned my salvation since the day He revealed Himself to me and I bowed my knee to live a life of service to my King. I have been accused of "blind faith" and even being "too simple" in my view of God. But interestingly enough, I do not have anxiety about my future with Jesus. Never have and probably never will because His foundation is solid within of me. I "know that I know" He has saved my soul from death and I am now in His family. It only becomes the daily pursuit for more revelation of this, a broader understanding and a settling of my mind and emotions, that causes me to daily push through until I receive the promise of my faith—eternal life.

During my short time on earth, these things have been brought to my attention: The rich, the high minded, the proud, and all other categories of humans who act openly as if they do not need God, are not the ones who hear the message of the Gospel easily. It is the sin nature that prevent us from hearing clearly. Less sin equals better hearing. Clear communication from God is a given.

Our soul, with all its faulty thinking and emotional responses to circumstances while in this body, causes the distortion of the clear channel from God through Holy Spirit. Our spirit man is not confused. He does not sin (1 John 5:18). So then let's make the effort to work on the things that cause us consternation, that make us miserable humans at times until we come to the full nature and stature of Christ (2 Peter 1:4).

I am convinced if we were on earth long enough, following the teaching and leading of the Holy Spirit, then we would be perfect without sin just like Jesus (Ephesians 4:13).

Be encouraged my brethren

We are not alone on earth, barely scratching out an understanding of the Holy One. We are His workmanship created in Christ for good works. We are the righteousness of God in Christ Jesus. We are complete in Him. We are accepted in the beloved.

We have been given all things that pertain to life and godliness. We are without excuse because we are His!

Live the life of God today from a willing heart

Love those around you as Jesus would do. Deny yourself when it is expedient. Give glory to our Father. Embrace Holy Spirit, act on the revelation of "what's on your screen" from Him and you will be prosperous and be in health even as your soul prospers. And above all things follow this commandment in Luke 10:27, "You shall love the Lord your God with all your heart, with all your soul, with all your strength, and with all your mind, and your neighbor as yourself. . . Do this and you will live."

**THE LOVE WALK ALWAYS
TRIUMPHS OVER EVIL.
GO ON WITH GOD.**

Glossary

New man — "born again being"
(Romans 6:22, 8:1, 14, 16. Ephesians 4:23-24, Colossians 3:10, 2 Peter 1:3-4, 1 John 2:29, 3:9, 5:4-5, 18).

Old man — "old self who died"
(Romans 6:6, 2 Corinthians 5:17, Colossians 3:7-9, Ephesians 4:20-22).

Holy Spirit Baptism — the experience of receiving "power from on high" to be witnesses in the earth that Jesus spoke of in Acts 1:8. Boldness and the supernatural manifestation of God and His gifts of the Spirit (1 Corinthians 12:7-11) are evident as a result of this baptism. Believers who receive this baptism are able to speak in a new language not known by their mind (1 Corinthians 14:2, 4, 14-18, 22, 28, 39). Also referred to as "filled with the Spirit" (Acts 9:17), "gift of the Holy Spirit" (Acts 8:20, 10:45, 11:15), "receiving the Holy Spirit" (Acts 10:47), "comforter" (John 14:16, 26), and referred to "fell on them" (Acts 11:15).